HALF A PACK OF
CIGS & A
LIGHTER THAT
DOESN'T WORK

DYLISIUM

Half a Pack of Cigs and a Lighter that Doesn't Work

Copyright © Linda Fragomeni, 2021

First published 2021
Published by Linda Fragomeni

Email: dylisium@gmail.com

All rights reserved. Without limiting the rights under copyright reserved above, no part of this publication may be reproduced, stored in or introduced into a database and retrieval system or transmitted in any form or any means (electronic, mechanical, photocopying, recording or otherwise) without the prior written permission of both the owner of copyright and the above publishers.

Original illustrations by Courtney Ellis

Half a Pack of Cigs and a Lighter that Doesn't Work

Dylisium

before entering into this book
i ask you to take note of some very serious
trigger warnings that may apply to you

keep in mind these trigger warnings if you are
buying this book as a gift for someone else

the pages to follow could trigger
anyone suffering or recovering from

addiction
suicidal tendencies
drug use
alcohol abuse
self-hatred
self-harm
domestic violence
heavily tainted with foul language

contents:

all these tears are so bad for my skin

before you go absolutely fucking nuts

don't mind me this is what i call living

the things that i think about are scary

you seem safe

if you're reading this book
then i guess it was meant for you...

and if you relate to this book
then i feel fucking sorry for you

all these tears are so bad for my skin

i hate to sound harsh but
fuck you
i hope you die
i can't believe what you said
i bet you thought you were clever
jumping in and out of her bed
i bet you thought i was fooled
reading her texts in the dark
grabbing her by the throat
and trying not to leave a mark
i hate you
i mean every word
i hope you choke on your lies
and when you tell her you're leaving
i fucking hope she cries

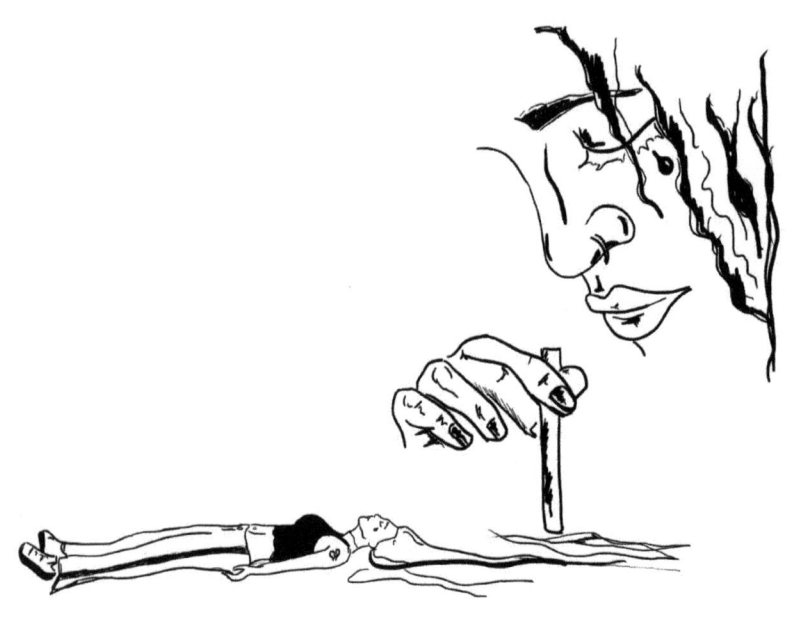

if i turned into powder
and fell to the floor
would you take me like a line
would it make you want me more

lie
cheat
deceive
beat me down until i'm a pulp
thoughts that cripple me
like wounds covered in salt

it's not okay
it never will be
it's never really done
lie to me you know i love
how it rolls off your tongue

uppers
downers
alcohol
numb me with foil and flames
around in perfect circles and memorised games

tell you the truth
tell you it hurts
tell you you're a piece of shit

i guess it doesn't matter
because you won't believe any of it

every letter
in every word you said
was coated with a lie
every space
between each word
was smothered too

played off like you were some born again saint
not sure if you think you're fooling me or you

tell me how i'm crazy
how it's all just in my head
and i'll tell you how i know
how many times you've been in her bed

thinking about you makes me feel sick
that's right i said
vomit
puke
be sick
spit up
hurl
chuck
spit chunks
choke until i can't breathe anymore

i hope that reading this makes you feel the same
because that's how i feel
anytime someone mentions
your name

is not replying to me
your best tactic of abuse

is accidentally hurting someone really a thing

you tell me stories
i can't relate
must be because
i'm not heartless

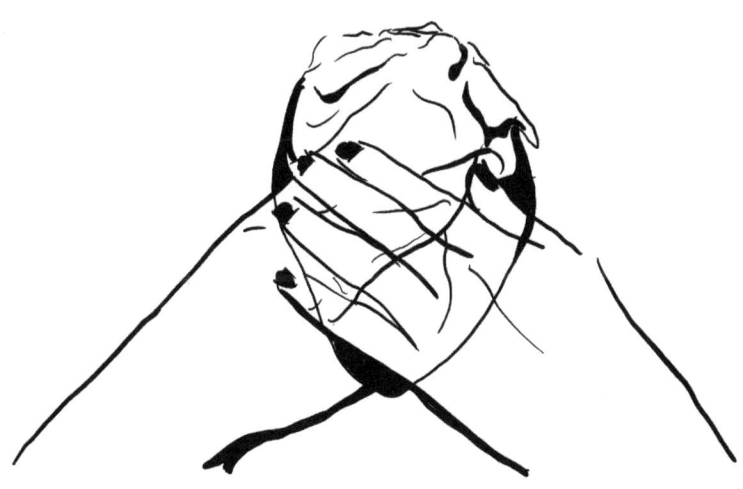

temporary
disposable
all because of you

hide from me
lie to me
i haven't got a clue

irrelevant
invalid
you literally mean shit

fucked it up
fucked me over
you couldn't fucking resist

just a liar
can't deny her
of everything she asks for
i'm such a bore
adhering to her every
stupid
fucking
word

i guess a part of me wants you to be happy
doesn't everyone deserve happiness
but much more of me wants you to

suffer
feel pain
agony
hurt
betrayal
useless
worthless
not enough
vile
disgusted
disappointed
invalid
irrelevant
replaceable
temporary

to feel like it's never going to get better
and everything is hopeless

because that's how you make me feel

i didn't mean for you to go and fuck up everything

you're the biggest liar i've ever met
the biggest thing i'll ever regret
preach me your loyalty lie to my face
you just look pathetic you fucking disgrace
words that prove nothing you're just useless
just the thought of you makes me feel putrid
do things you know will fucking kill me
plead and beg to be the one who will heal me
i kill you every day in my mind
nothing about you is slightly divine
you're gross, foul, not worth a second of time
disgusted at myself for ever calling you mine
i think about waking up to watch you suffer
i hate you i said i didn't fucking stutter
forget you're a cunt
when you're painting my name
play your sadistic psychotic
deranged stupid game
act like an angel you vulgar hypocrite
then talk about me like i'm a monster
i'm fucking used to it

inhale me
then fail me
taint every word with deceit
till you speak
and i never believe
a word you choose to say

i don't like writing about you
but i still do it

the difference is now i only write about you
on pages that can be torn out
and notes that can be deleted

because
i never
want to
remember you

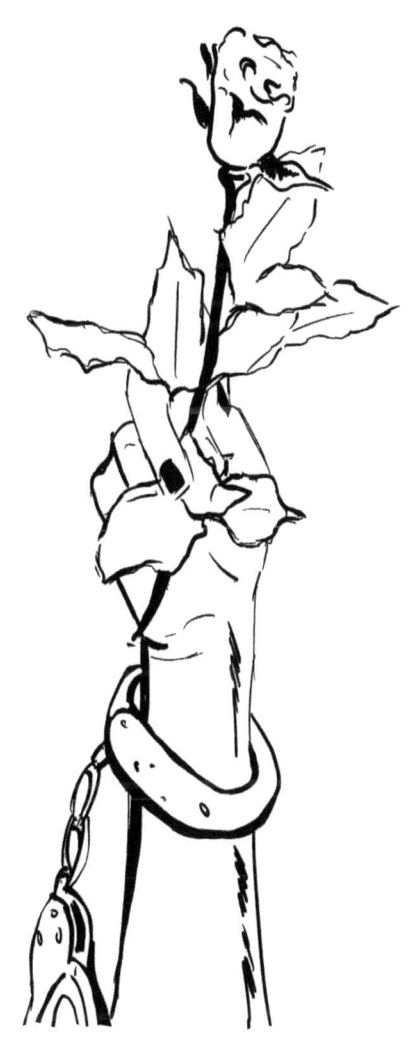

i can't breathe you killed me
go and turn yourself in

lost everything she was
chasing everything i wanted
and she succeeded

got it
loved it
abused it
killed it
all for her own pleasure
i'm better

picking up her pieces as usual
now it's my mess
she got undressed
not me
not surprised
just more lies

no truth in anything
it doesn't exist
it's fiction
doesn't stop my addiction
it's her

i'm her key to happiness
but she's unaware
too busy dancing
in her drug lair

all these tears are so bad for my skin

secret messages behind her back
to save her heart
tear it apart
rip it to shreds
i simply don't care

pushing the edge of losing her
abusing her
using her
but i need her

shared a love
broke my heart

sorry's said
forgiveness offered
all contrived
more fucking lies

she's a cunt
i'm a cunt
both wanting the same sort of crazy
to fuck up our lives

killing each other piece by piece
to get a taste of the same psycho

i simply don't fucking care

fuck the system
fuck the bitching
fuck the liars
fuck the bullshit
fuck everyone
fuck everything
fuck anything
fuck you

i'm sorry should have never come from my lips, it should have come from yours. sometimes i sit back, think of all the things you did to me and wonder how i can even speak your name. i thought i'd take a moment to remind you of the top hits that really made the charts in those 3 years

the time i walked in on you in the toilets with her
the time you kissed my best friend
the time you spent the day with a girl and told me you were at home
the time you shot up speed with my ex gf
the time you dropped me to a festival alone so you could get high
the time you started messaging that girl from nsw
the time i found out you cheated because of a photo on a facebook page
the time you left me a drunk voicemail meant for someone else
the time i introduced you to my friends and you fucked one of them
the time you went missing on new years and i found you in bed with him
the time you got angry because i wouldn't go to sleep so you could fuck my housemate

no it never should have been me to say sorry
i guess i'm sorry i ever loved you

before you go absolutely fucking nuts

i totalled myself today
need to stop thinking about you this way

you're weak you know
weak weak weak
cry baby, pushover, piece of shit weak

tell women to stand up for themselves
you can't even stand up for yourself

you're pathetic, a loser, a fake, disgraceful
you'll never be a role model

who would want to look up to someone
who crumbles so easily

threw your strength out the door
the second you let down your walls

you're fucking weak

she thinks i'm okay cause i smile
haven't tried to kill myself in awhile
take three 25mg just to drown it out
she wouldn't even know what i'm talking about
put pen to paper to try and release it
it's all i've got when i can't speak it
one secret 1 litre bottle of red
to fight it off so i can go to fucking bed
3 more 25mg maybe now i'll pass out
i guess not even i know
what the fuck i'm talking about

i love you like i love myself which isn't very much

i threw a party on my front lawn for you
the only person there was me
cigarette in my right hand
and a heart that just wanted to bleed

there's a crowd that cheers inside of my head
anytime that i think i'd rather be dead

i don't think you meant it
when you said you missed me

fucked it
what did i expect
did i really think
i was better than this

getting faded
chasing wasted
anything to forget
cause i regret
what i've done

full of shit
spitting bullshit
to save face
cause i'm a waste
of any space

oh my god
what the fuck
have i done

dying by the hands of your lying love
because it's all i ever lived for

i stayed up for you
because i thought you were worth it
countless shots and cigarette shops
until the sun rose while we sat on the stairs

i stayed up for you because you were my main
not the same as anyone else
worth every second of exhaustion

i stayed up for you but not on purpose
my body just wouldn't let me sleep
when it knew what you were doing

i stayed up for you while you slept sound
every lie i found on replay in my mind
only a matter of time before it all came out

i stayed up for you
but only so i could keep drinking
barricades smokes and endless days
to stop the consistent thinking

i stayed up for you out of force of habit
i never sleep anymore
memories of staring at the door
waiting for you to walk through at 5am

i stayed up for you hoping
my acceptance was never enough
what a tough lesson to learn
that not everything is so fucking easy

another note about you
get a grip
don't slip
she isn't worth the attention

you smell like nostalgia it's pleasant
you taste like regret it's revolting

none of it meant a single thing
until it became a memory
you don't mean anything to me

ill-gotten gains
mind fucked games
only hatred remains
i'm fucking insane

a thousand words one million ways
still none of it makes sense

time wasted
time spent
nothing to believe in
i'm leaving

and still you find reasons not to love me

panic attacks and distorted views
but what do i do
when it's all that's left
that reminds me of you

i had visions of everything
turning out so beautifully
but all i got in return
was an ending so brutal to me

i'd hoped not to be reminded
of everything i once let go
but you showed me that hell still exists
in everyone i'll ever know

i don't dwell or cry
i've got happiness on my side
i watch you tear her down to shreds
and i watch you laugh when she cries

every bone in my body wants to save her
instead of letting her be
but more than wanting to be the hero
i'm just so fucking thankful it isn't me

if the world thinks
i'm strong enough
to handle this
it's fucked

some days i want nothing more
than to come home to you
waiting for me in the driveway
with that 10/10 smile on your face
and to grab you
and feel you hug me so tight
that i struggle to say
baby i can't breathe

other days i want nothing more
than for you to make me feel like shit
grab me and throw me to the ground
yell at me and hit me so hard
that i struggle to say
baby i can't breathe

ultimately i want nothing more than you
however you come
until i can't breathe

she told me stories
that would make a human cringe
but for me i was captivated
all it did was draw me in

gluttony
that's the only reason you ever cared
dared you to show me something real
at first you did like it wasn't a big deal
but it was a lie

how long can you fool someone
about 5 months
then the truth starts to reveal
everything concealed

pulled you apart
showed you had no heart
only green for what anyone else wanted

fought for it
got it
juggled it
dropped it

and the worst is
you never even wanted it

maybe i'm scared because i'm used to this
maybe i'm scared cause i don't know what this is
maybe i'm scared cause you treat me like shit
maybe i'm scared cause you make me feel sick
maybe i don't want you to leave
maybe you should so i can breathe
maybe you give me nothing to believe
maybe you give me something to deceive
maybe one day you'll stop keeping me awake
maybe you're the reason i'm in such a state
maybe you're my worst and biggest mistake
maybe you're the definition of the word hate

intrigued by me
deceived by me
had you thinking i was worthless

enthused by me
confused by me
made you think i came with a purpose

repulsed by you
disgusted by you
had me thinking maybe you weren't the same

sickened by you
buried by you
made me think things were going to change

lied to each other
blinded each other
i don't think we even knew what for

fooling each other
killing each other
i don't want to do this anymore

vacant as hell when i look in your eyes
and they used to be as full as heaven

putrid the way that we used to lie
left each other bleeding and begging

paranoid now
i don't know what's right or what the fuck to do

blessed to no longer love the disease that is you

nothing is real and neither are you
illusion
confusion
all of it untrue

one lie here
a secret there
hiding everything
completely not scared

waking with a smile
but sleep isn't the same
addicted to things
that constantly change

sunshine and happiness
storms and rain
infected my memory
diseased and in pain

up and down insane
drew a line and i've crossed it

holy shit
i've truly fucking lost it

i wrote about you but i wont post it
couldn't bare for you to see my thoughts
it would remind you of why you liked me
and how you miss the way we talked

the words for you they never die
it's like a gathering of letters forever
sentences and pages of all the reasons
we aren't ever together

the thoughts they don't exist very much
i've moved on and into clearer views
and there's not much space
but there's still a little place
where i can sit when i do think about you

and i wrote about you but i wont post it
i would never want you to see
just how much i'm not missing you
the way you're not missing me

you pretend you don't care
and i pretend i don't notice

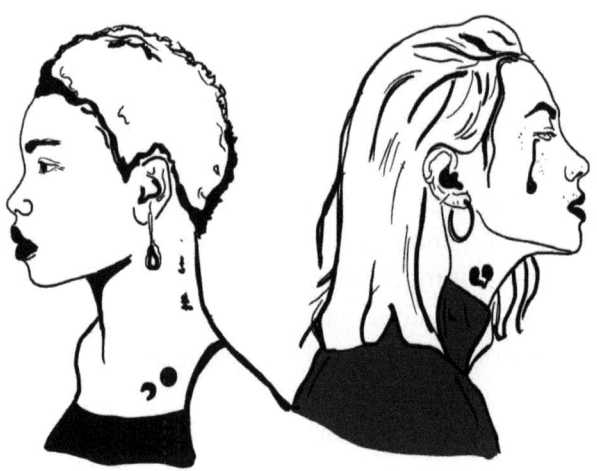

i can't stand the way
you notice every other girl in the room
but fail to notice me

i can't stand how every word you say
makes me hate every word i say

i can't stand how i stand here
and accept the sick you throw at me
with open arms

i can't stand the alcohol you drink
the cigarettes you smoke
the pills i take to deal with the fact
we exist at the same time

i can't stand anything about you

it's not even a missing you feeling
it's more of an empty
empty message notifications
empty glasses, no its empty bottles
empty passenger seats
empty morning messages
empty tables for two
empty futures
empty fucking everything
you piece of god damn shit
fuck you
fuck you
fuck you
fuck you
fucking god damn fuck you
fuck it

you made me hate
long hair
blonde hair
ripped thighs
blue eyes
not because they remind me of you
because they remind me of
who you left me for

unpack your thoughts
out of little boxes
into little piles
give them time
sort them out
before you go
absolutely
fucking
nuts

you never looked at me with vacant eyes
that's how i got confused
got used
and abused
and the whole time i enjoyed it

thought you were winning
cause i let you keep grinning
but i gave you permission to tear me apart
so i could feel something

it wasn't you who picked me up when i called
rescued me when i bawled
or even made me feel happy

it got fun getting drunk when you weren't around
didn't feel so bound
yelling wasn't a sound
and everything was peaceful

i feel an unusual sense of free
when i push you away
and try but fail to forget you

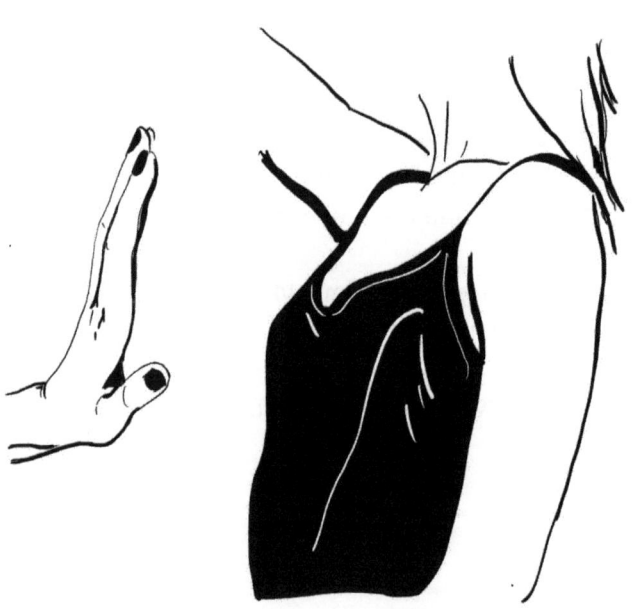

it's boring and i promised
id never do this again
put my pen to paper and hoped it would end

always empty going through the motions
anything is better than solving these emotions

ignore it
destroy it
push it aside
i sighed and i cried because i knew the answer

drowning in red talking to myself
deteriorating my own mental health

pseudoephedrine that's where i've been
and i hope that i never come back

i sat waiting in the pouring rain
but you never noticed
so i opened a bottle of wine
thinking it would make me less nervous
i guess it worked
you grabbed a glass and joined me for awhile
lied to me
then said sorry
thinking it would make me smile
got up once you'd done your worst
left me alone again
kicked me as you walked away
told me i needed to mend

i told you i was okay
because you'd get tired of hearing how i'm not

you're just always leaving
for someone else's time
and i'm just always waiting
wasting all of my time

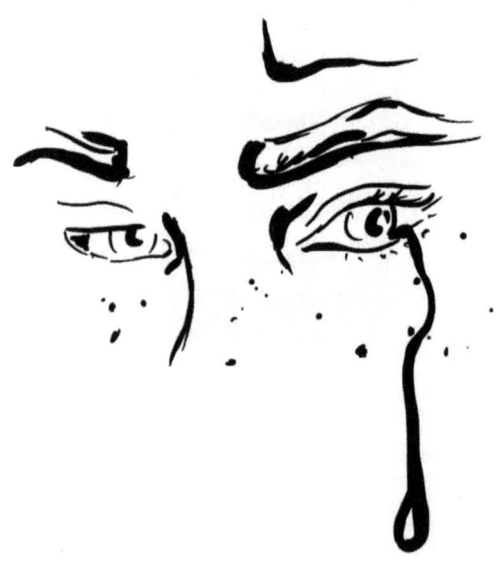

as i stop laying my pencil to paper
to spill words about you
i realise every song i've ever cared for before
wasn't written about him or her
it's about loss
but not of a person
the loss of addiction
alcohol
cigarettes
drugs
freedom
heroin
pills
freedom
whiskey
did i say fucking freedom
and without any words left to write about you
i guess i'll start writing about these things too
cause they're the only things i miss anymore

don't mind me this is what i call living

didn't realise i was so foul
until i read what i wrote about you

don't even know what you did
to make my guts spill venom at you

every bad word i've ever known
painted beside your name
unleashed every evil in me
never to be tamed

felt it
spat it
stomped it
crushed it
killed it then fucked it up

still don't know if i regret it
or if it was all just bad luck

how much more can i take
before it defeats me
there is nothing
that will ever complete me

old hotel rooms
that cost too much money
are the only thing now
that remind me of you honey

still made beds
cause we never fell asleep
when you said that you had to leave next week

hearts that fell
right through the floor
i told you i didn't want to live anymore

stared at you
for the next 7 days
you grabbed my hand and pulled me away

downed a shot, did a line, lit a smoke
both of us forgetting we were broke

with shattered glass ripping up both my hands
i picked you up to try help you to stand

packed it in and joined you down on the floor
and you told me....

you didn't want to live anymore

there's an unfinished drink
laying somewhere in a gutter

with half a pack of cigs
and a lighter that doesn't work

and its waiting for us to return

i guess one day we'll no longer wonder
we would have solved the question
of why we spent so long
screaming at each other
to see who could hurt the most
without leaving a mark
i wonder
if after that day
i'll still drink every night to forget you

it's easier not to tell you what i think
instead ill just drink
and sink
and drown
until i forget what it was i couldn't tell you

will somebody get me a drink
i'm pretty done with being sober now
i don't know how i ever dealt with it before

3 months since i've had valium
used to have them everyday
i'm not okay

no one actually gets it
they say they do

think it's fun
to be the one
who always drinks
and downs the scripts
get a grip

but what else am i going to do
when i'd rather be drunk and high
than ever remember you

i wonder if the things i taught you
you teach her
and pretend they're from your mind
and not mine

i got drunk again
took prescription meds again
don't mind me this is what i call living

i got fucked again
took those words to heart again
don't mind me i was just reliving

i got used again
took actions for truths again
don't mind me i was just forgetting

i fell in love again
burnt the memories we made again
don't mind me i was still forgetting

i worked it out again
knew better won't be a fool again
don't mind me i was just regretting

i downed that shot again
smoked glass to erase again
don't mind me just forever regretting

i hope you're kissing other girls now
i hope that you don't love them

my head it ruins everything
see it makes up these stories
these stories of terror
full of bad weather and pain

it fills up my mind
with death threats and lies
so real i believe them and every inch of me cries

make me happy
give it your best shot
i've lost the plot

i guarantee you won't succeed
it's a mess in there and i can't sort it out
all i know is hatred and self-doubt

still try if you want
try something
try anything
just don't get disappointed when you lose

because my head it ruins everything

i miss feeling things that i hated feeling
i miss the person i thought i was
i miss drinking alone to clear my head
i miss having nothing to care about
i miss everything i hated
i mis-understood everything

i only miss you
when you're standing next to me
i only feel you
when you're no-where near me
i only understand you
when you're not making any sense
i only trust you
when you're spitting lies
i only love you
when you don't love me

my heart caught fire for you
at first it kept me warm
but after awhile
all it did was make me burn

there's this song that reminds me of you
when i'm alone all i do is play it

i don't know why
i don't cry
i was thankful for goodbye
it makes no sense

i know i'm just your regret
made you upset
wish to forget human
i wouldn't want to be more

truth be told i grew to loathe you
i still do

hearing your name makes my insides turn
brings a sickness in my throat

still there's this song that makes me think of you
when i'm alone all i do is play it

i'll get drunk and say things i can't when i'm sober
and ill mean every word
but tell you i don't remember
in case you're not feeling it
don't want to deal with that temper
because it's easier when you're fucked
who cares whatever
and i despise that you exist but what the fuck ever

can't fall asleep with a heart so heavy
can't fall asleep wanting you
thinking about
how much more i can destroy myself
to impress you

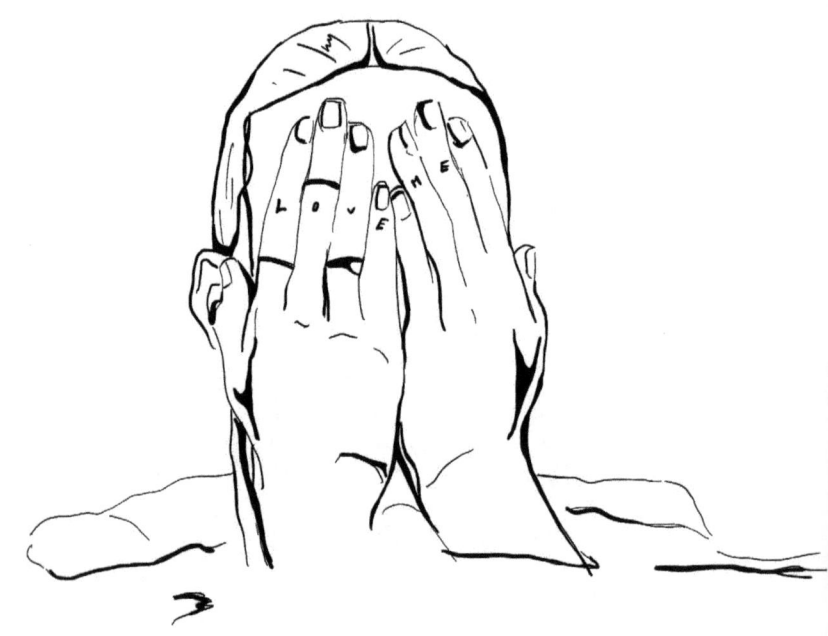

a dream to remember you
as more than what you did to me

i think about you in colours
colours changed when you arrived
colours changed when you left
i think about you

i think about you in lies that will never be truths
i think about you

i think about you in kisses that don't exist
beds that never mess
stories that are never told

i think about you yesterday
today
but not tomorrow

i think about me
i think about you
i just do

two damaged hearts don't make a right

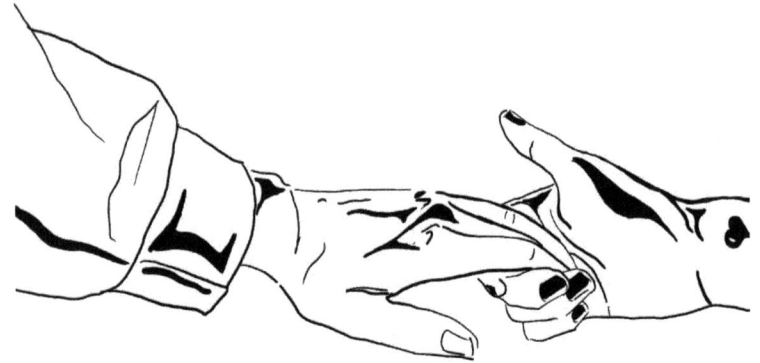

your chaos was my peace
that's the only reason you made me weak

the things that i think about are scary

just me and the red and the voices in my head

the things that i think about are scary
but i can't let them scare me
the things that they talk about are boring
but i can't let it make them abhorrent

unintentionally surrounded by things
that don't entice me

this is precisely
everything i didn't want

i still wish that it wasn't like this
i'm still free but i didn't want it like this
i still wake but it's never in my bed
i'm still alive but i'd rather be dead
i still hope that naivety exists
i'm still weighed down with your every wish
i still hate every lie i've ever told
i still regret letting myself grown old
i still know that i'm completely full of shit
i no longer fucking care about any of it

i'm sure i wrote this for someone
but i have no idea who

destroy it
every single part
and once destroyed i wonder
does it get better
or worse
destroying it opens up
feeling
hating
fucking
arguing
hurting
liking
killing
but keeping it
well it simply means
you're safe

i only see in black and white, occasionally grey,

never colour

an assortment of garbage
that someone has tried to save

strangers are heaven
they don't expect
they don't know
they don't want

you can be the deepest
foulest
nicest
version of yourself
they accept it
because they don't know any other you

strangers are heaven
because i can be whoever i want to be
and that suits me fine
when i wish i was somebody else

stiff drinks remind me
it's okay to want to forget
lies remind me
i don't believe truths anymore
compliments make me remember
i'm a piece of shit
friends remind me
freedom comes at a price
suffocating reminds me
loneliness should be appreciated
being sorry reminds me
that i failed even though i tried
enemies reassure me
some people see me for what i am
mornings remind me
i still haven't escaped you
and when i miss you less
it hurts me more
because it reminds me
nothing is forever

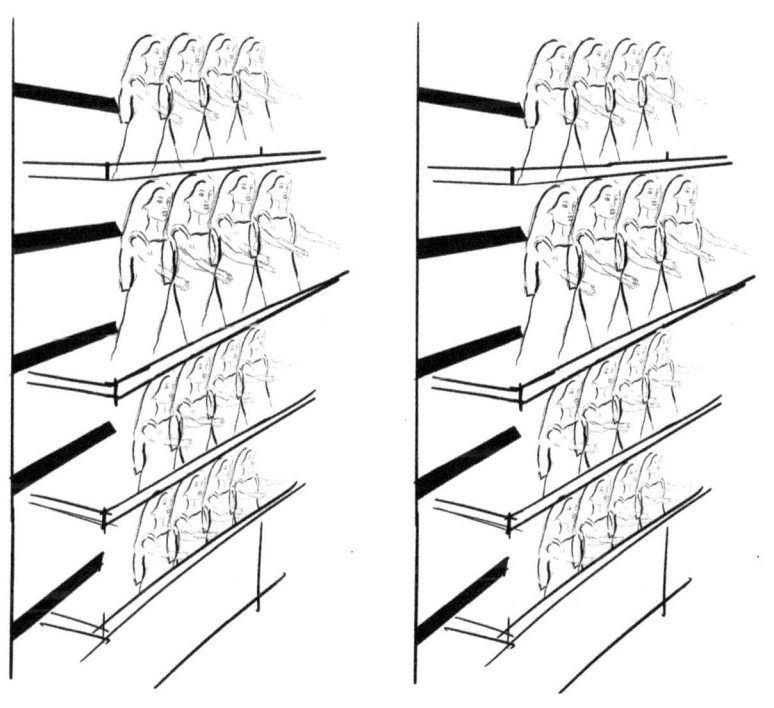

who the fuck are you
to judge anyone else
you're just a pre-packaged person
straight from the shelf

just tell me what you hate

and i promise i won't change

i guess i don't care
i don't feel
if i do i don't share
i don't think
i don't give a fucking shit
i don't learn
i don't care about any of this
i don't wish
i definitely don't dream
i don't love
i don't think you're what you seem

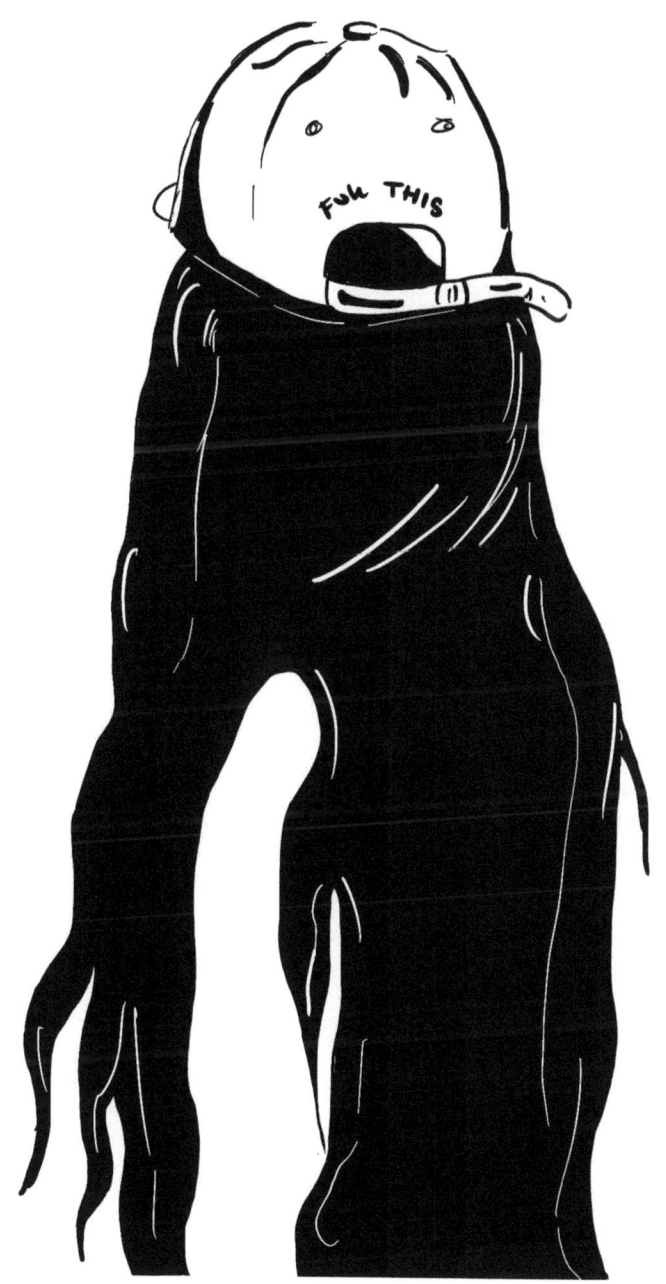

what is it
is it pretty colours
chirpy songs
holding hands
and cheek kisses

is it
dark colours
abhorrent songs
choking me
and shoving your fingers down my throat

is it
black eyes
and spilled red veins
vulgar poetry
with last night's wine
carrying me home
hitting me hard
and shoving your fingers inside me
when i tell you i'm not good enough
but you ignore me anyway

what the fuck is it

she comes with warning signs
for those of you that need them

dear future human

i love you

weirdly enough i do, even though i never wanted to, even though i hadn't imagined a future with a person, i for some reason love you

i love how you wake up in the morning and you're the perfect amount of mess to make me smile just a little at how unperfect you are. i love how you know me well enough to get a bunch of winter earth tone flowers instead of roses when you want to surprise me. i love how intently you listen when i rant and when i get truly into it you can't help but smile a little and laugh at how insane i am. i love how i don't have to ask, what would you like, wherever we go because i already know your every single order for every single venue

i love how we bail on going out so we can sit in the park and get drunk on wine and smoke cheap cigarettes and talk about stars. i love how even when we do go out i'll catch your gaze from across the room and you'll roll your eyes to let me know how uninteresting the smoking area banter girl you're listening to is and i'll laugh and mouth, good luck babe

i love how you know when to run me a bath and have lana playing to calm me down i love how when you compliment me you make sure it's always on my personality and if you must compliment me on my looks, i love how i know you're doing it to build me up

i love how on tuesdays i'll sit and watch your favourite tv show with you, even though i don't like tv

i love how every second alone is worth it because one day i'll get to look at you and say
i love you

future human

you seem safe

i think about you

then i think i just need to go to sleep
and tomorrow ill wake up and not think about you

it never works

you seem safe
it's because of that lack of danger
that you're so dangerous

do i want it, i don't know
do i need it, i hope not
do i feel it, i think so
is it worth it, i'm not sure
are you playing the fool, yes
will you fuck it up, definitely

i asked you not to leave
stay lost within my sheets
let me stay in my daydream
where you can always be seen
i don't care to beg
i'll stay silent in bed
it's not over there
eyes close and you're everywhere
i'm lost but i'm not naive

painted on my eyelids, but i can't see you
screaming at my chest, but i can't hear you
clawing at my skin, but i can't feel you
poisoning my drinks, but i can't taste you
writing pretty words, but i can't read you
throwing everything you've got
but i won't catch you

you.

i think i could love you and that's heavy as fuck

used to things falling to shit
right now they're coming together
like a piece of writing that i read repeatedly
but never made sense
turning into a song that i know
every lyric off by heart

you're not the type of poetry
that i could have learnt
or read from friends

you're the type that keeps me awake at night
repeating over and over again
words too deep to initially comprehend

i traded poison for passion and i won
i understand

come over, come and lay on my bed
listen to me talk
about everything and nothing all at the same time
we can waste hours saying
what should we do today
when we both have no intentions
of leaving the dim lit, vanilla scented, unmade bed

carry me home, carry me to the front door
after you've got me drunk enough
to talk about all the things i won't when i'm sober
the i thinks
the i wishes
the i feels
acting like it's awkward and i want to leave
but i have no intention of getting up
from this grey coloured, unnoticed, secret filled chair of
a front porch step

you asked me if i could feel it
and i said
i can't feel anything else

coffee tastes better with you
sitting across from me
whinging about how there isn't enough
chocolate in your mocha
to drown out the coffee taste in yours

cooking feels better with you
when you sit cross legged on the floor next to me
and talk shit while we watch the food
in the oven cook

drinking works better with you
when you pick me up after i fall
and laugh at my pathetic existence
with your hand on my leg
when you drink drive us home

drugs feel better with you
when we are down at the beach
sharing a million thoughts in complete silence
ending the night with a simple hand gesture, cool

living feels better with you
for now i guess
and if it fails then at least i'll always have
hot mochas
kitchen floors
alcohol
beaches
and cool
to remind me of you

you make my mind go from
ncjskdjxhbdsnskjdhbaakhhknk
to

_____

i didn't used to see many bad places
but even the small few i did
disappeared as you appeared

you make me wish for things
i gave up wishing for a long time ago

you show me a version of me
i thought didn't exist anymore

i still don't believe in anything
but if i did it would be you

love isn't real
it's just something that we believe in
the only place it exists
is when we're daydreaming

so forgive me for never saying that i love you
it just isn't something i think i'll ever want to do

i don't write much about you
i've tried to work out why

i don't write about you because of fear
you're the only thing i don't know

i know hurt and heartache
like the back of my hand
like lana del rey lyrics on red vinyl
like camp cope songs in the corolla
i know these things like the back of my hand

i don't know love like you
i can write about the failure that haunts me
about the people i loathe
about the times i miss
because they're what i'm used to

i'm not used to loves that last
and things that don't have a past

i don't know you

i thought everyone was temporary
i guess i still do
you seem to be more than momentary

you keep telling me
you're going to be here forever
like it'll make me better

i don't think anything will ever be okay
but at least i know when i'm
drowning
thinking
drinking
that you'll stay

the lines on your arms
even though you tried to cover them up
tell me you had feelings that you want to hide
i don't make you talk about them
i'm just aware you're not what you seem
the first time you said you loved me might have been
when you were drunk in a room full of boys over a ping
pong table but it couldn't have been more perfect
we took pills and i blacked out but i remember sitting at
the beach with you listening to shitty aussie bands and
holding your hand
woke up in byron singing keep growing and
ended up at footscray station
it was late nights in cinema car parks
secret key rings
pub bathrooms
playgrounds
shared music
kitchen floors
kitchen benches
hidden kisses
and lies that grew our foundation
every message i ever sent you
never went unanswered
even when i was plastered and made no sense
treated you like shit
still you didn't quit
i don't know how to thank you

i lost myself
when you weren't home
even though you were still in my arms
i hated myself
but still loved you
and every decision was doing us harm
parked my car and cried
somewhere on the side of the road
end it now it hurts
please don't make me go home
i found myself
when you found you
and we fell back in love again
but ill hate myself
if we fuck it up
and i have to feel losing you again

i don't want to marry you today
but i'll do it anyway

not because you're not the one
because the one isn't real

not because you're not a lot
because by god you're consuming

not because you're not happiness
because that's all you've ever shown me

not because you're not heaven
because you made heaven exist

i don't want to marry you today
because if i do

i'm just like everybody else

and still everyday you're on my mind

there just isn't anything to write about anymore
i'm unsure if that's good
or terrifying....

Lightning Source UK Ltd.
Milton Keynes UK
UKHW021054221221
396076UK00009B/760